COMPLETE
PIANO SONATAS

ALEXANDER SCRIABIN

COMPLETE PIANO SONATAS

DOVER PUBLICATIONS, INC., *New York*

Published in Canada by General Publishing Company, Ltd., 30 Lesmill Road, Don Mills, Toronto, Ontario.

Published in the United Kingdom by Constable and Company, Ltd., 10 Orange Street, London WC2H 7EG.

This Dover edition, first published in 1988, is a republication of *A. Skrîabin, Sonaty dlîa fortepiano* (A. Scriabin, Sonatas for Piano), edited by K. N. Igumnov and Yȃ. I. Mil'šteĭn (Sonatas 1–4) and L. N. Oborin and Yȃ. I. Mil'šteĭn (Sonatas 5–10), and published by [Gosudarstvennoe Izdatel'stvo] "Muzyka" (State Music Publishing House), Moscow, 1964. The footnotes, epigraph to Sonata 5, and table of contents have been translated into English. The publisher is grateful to the Paddock Music Library, Department of Music, Dartmouth College, Hanover, New Hampshire, for lending the music for reproduction.

Manufactured in the United States of America
Dover Publications, Inc., 31 East 2nd Street, Mineola, N.Y. 11501

Library of Congress Cataloging-in-Publication Data

Scriabin, Aleksandr Nikolayevich, 1872–1915.
  [Sonatas, piano]
  Complete piano sonatas.

  Reprint. Originally published: Sonaty dlia fortepiano. Moscow : Muzyka, 1964.
  Contents: No. 1 in F minor, op. 6 (1892)—No. 2 in G-sharp minor, op. 19 (1892–97) : Sonata-fantasy—No. 3 in F-sharp minor, op. 23 (1897–98)—[etc.]
  1. Sonatas (Piano)   I. Title.
M23.S628I3   1988   88-753352
ISBN 0-486-25850-5

� Contents

🍃 Glossary of French Terms in Sonatas 6 through 10

ailé, tourbillonnant, winged, spinning; *animé, ailé*, lively, winged; *appel mystérieux*, mysterious call; *avec éclat*, brilliantly; *avec élan*, with dash; *avec élan lumineux, vibrant*, with luminous, vibrant élan; *avec émotion*, with emotion; *avec entraînement*, with energy; *avec ravissement*, with rapture; *avec ravissement et tendresse*, with rapture and tenderness; *avec trouble*, worried; *avec une ardeur profonde et voilée*, with deep, veiled ardor; *avec une céleste volupté*, with heavenly voluptuousness; *avec une chaleur contenue*, with restrained warmth; *avec une douce ivresse*, with gentle intoxication; *avec une douce langueur de plus en plus éteinte*, with gentle languor that is more and more extinguished; *avec une douceur de plus en plus caressante et empoisonnée*, with a gentleness more and more caressing and poisoned; *avec une joie débordante*, with excessive joy; *avec une joie exaltée*, with exultation; *avec une joie subite*, with sudden joy; *avec une joyeuse exaltation*, with exalted joy; *avec une langueur naissante*, with incipient languor; *avec une sombre majesté*, darkly majestic; *avec une volupté douloureuse*, with painful voluptuousness; *avec une volupté radieuse, extatique*, with radiant, ecstatic voluptuousness; *charmes*, charms; *comme des éclairs*, like flashes of lightning; *concentré*, concentrated; *cristallin*, crystalline; *de plus en plus entraînant, avec enchantement*, more and more alluring, spellbinding; *de plus en plus radieux*, more and more radiant; *de plus en plus sonore et animé*, more and more sonorous and lively; *doux, languissant*, gentle, languishing; *effondrement subit*, sudden collapse; *en délire*, delirious; *en s'éteignant peu à peu*, dying away little by little; *en un vertige*, dizzily; *épanouissement de forces mystérieuses*, unfurling of mysterious powers; *étincelant*, sparkling; *étrange, ailé*, strange, winged; *frémissant, ailé*, trembling, winged; *foudroyant*, thunderous; *fulgurant*, dazzling; *haletant*, breathless; *impérieux*, imperious; *inquiet*, troubled; *joyeux, triomphant*, joyous, triumphant; *la mélodie bien marquée*, melody marcato; *légendaire*, as if reciting a legend; *l'épouvante surgit, elle se mêle a la danse délirante*, horror arises and mingles with the delirious dance; *le rêve prend forme (clarté, douceur, pureté)*, the dream takes shape (brightness, gentleness, purity); *lumineux, vibrant*, luminous, vibrant; *menaçant*, threatening; *modéré*, moderato; *mystérieusement murmuré*, in a mysterious murmur; *mystérieusement sonore*, mysteriously sonorous; *mystérieux, concentré*, mysterious, concentrated; *onde caressante*, caressing wave; *ondoyant*, in waves; *onduleux, insinuant*, undulous, insinuating; *puissant, radieux*, powerful, radiant; *pur, limpide*, pure, limpid; *sombre, mystérieux*, gloomy, mysterious; *souffle mystérieux*, mysterious breath; *tout devient charme et douceur*, becoming all charm and gentleness; *tragique*, tragically; *très animé, ailé*, very lively, winged; *très doux et pur*, very gentle and pure; *très doux, joyeux, étincelant*, very gentle, joyous, sparkling; *très pur, avec douceur*, very pure, gently; *très pur, avec une profonde douceur*, very pure, with profound gentleness; *un peu plus lent*, a little slower; *vol joyeux*, joyous flight.

COMPLETE
PIANO SONATAS

[1] Sonata No. 1 in F Minor, Op. 6

Allegro con fuoco M.M. ♩.=104

1) Scriabin's sketchbook contains the following notice, which characterizes his spiritual state at the time of composing the sonata: "20 years old: the injury to my hand has developed. The most important event in my life. Fate sends me forth on my mission. The obstacle to the achievement of the goal so highly desired: fame, glory. An obstacle, in the words of the doctors, that is insuperable. The first serious failure in my life. The first serious meditation: the beginning of analysis. Doubts about the impossibility of getting well, but the gloomiest state of mind. The first meditation on the value of life, on religion, on God. A continuing strong belief in Him (Sabaoth more than Christ, it seems). Ardent, heartfelt prayer, visits to church . . . Grumbling against fate and against God. Composition of my first sonata with a funeral march."

molto rit.

Presto M.M. ♩=132

p

cresc.

dim.

simile

4)

cresc.

dim.

sf

sf *sf*

sf

4)? (by analogy with mm. 1, 2, and 5 on this page).

una corda

5)?  (by analogy with a number of subsequent mm.). Scriabin himself, when performing similar triplets in other compositions, frequently changed the last eighth-note to a sixteenth-note.

6)? (by analogy with m. 8 from the end of this movement).

7)? 〄 (by analogy with m. 4 from the end of the movement).

Sonata No. 2 (Sonata-Fantasy) in G-sharp Minor, Op. 19

ben marcato il canto

Sonata No. 3 in F-sharp Minor, Op. 23

I

II

Allegretto M.M. ♪=160

III

Andante M.M. ♪ = 63

IV

Presto con fuoco M.M. $\quad \boldsymbol{\mathit{d}}.=58$

*) This passage, difficult to perform at a rapid tempo, was played differently by Scriabin himself:

etc.

[Tempo I]

Sonata No. 4 in F-sharp Major, Op. 30

I

II

Prestissimo volando M.M. ♩=160

80   Sonata No. 4

Sonata No. 5, Op. 53

„Я к жизни призываю вас, скрытые стремленья!„
Вы, утонувшие в темных глубинах
Духа творящего, вы, боязливые
Жизни зародыши, вам дерзновенье я приношу.„

(*Поэма экстаза, стр. 11*)

"I summon you to life, secret yearnings!
You who have been drowned in the dark depths
Of the creative spirit, you timorous
Embryos of life, it is to you that I bring daring."

(*Poem of Ecstasy*, 11)

Prestissimo

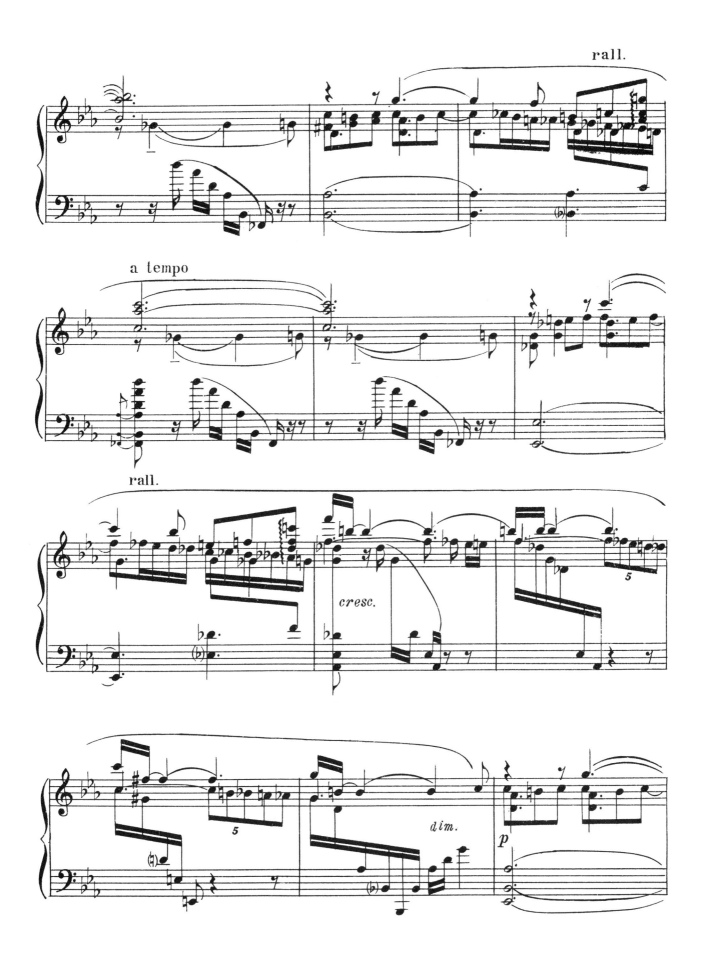

molto rall.

Allegro   accel.   poco   a   poco

P con una ebbrezza fantastica

vertiginoso con furia

*) If need be [OR, Strictly speaking], this note can be omitted. (Scriabin's observation.)

Sonata No. 6, Op. 62

le rêve prend forme (clarté, douceur, pureté)

ailé, tourbillonnant

l'épouvante surgit

Sonata No. 6   119

poco più vivo

appel mystérieux

de plus en plus entrainant, avec enchantement

charmes

poco cresc.

joyeux, triomphant

joyeux

appel
mystérieux

tout devient charme et douceur

poco cresc.

avec entrainement

ailé, tourbillonnant

l'épouvante surgit, elle se mele à la danse délirante

Sonata No. 7 ("White Mass"), Op. 64

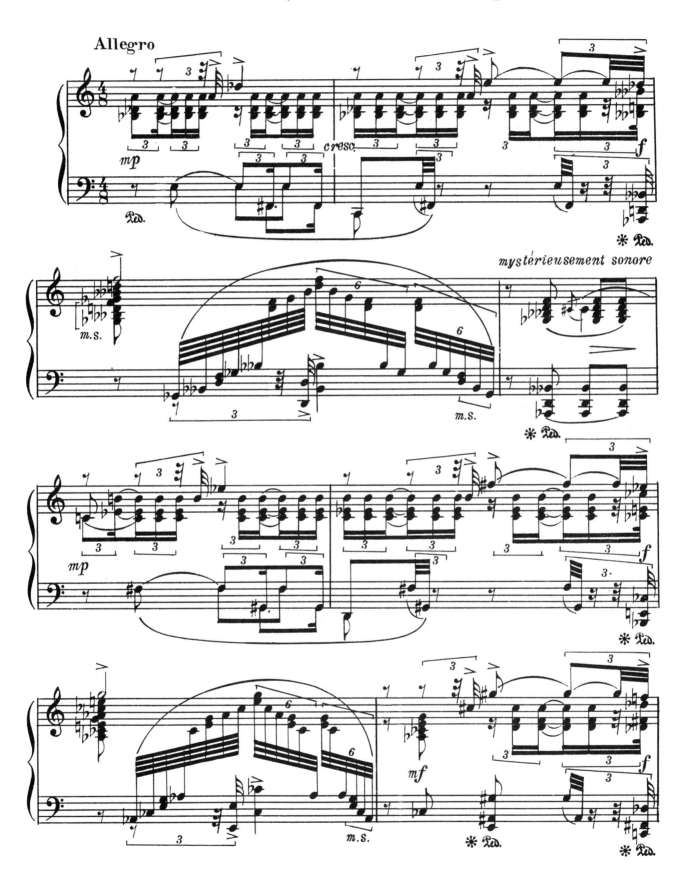

Poco meno vivo

très animé, ailé

pp

étincelant

pp

m.d.

cresc.

m.d.

148   Sonata No. 7 ("White Mass")

Sonata No. 7 ("White Mass")

avec une celeste volupté

tres pur, avec une profonde douceur

mystérieusement sonore

poco meno vivo

158   Sonata No. 7 ("White Mass")

Sonata No. 7 ("White Mass")

166   Sonata No. 7 ("White Mass")

Sonata No. 8, Op. 66

Tragique

178   Sonata No. 8

Tragique. Molto più vivo

182   Sonata No. 8

Allegro

Molto più vivo. Agitato

Allegro (Tempo I)

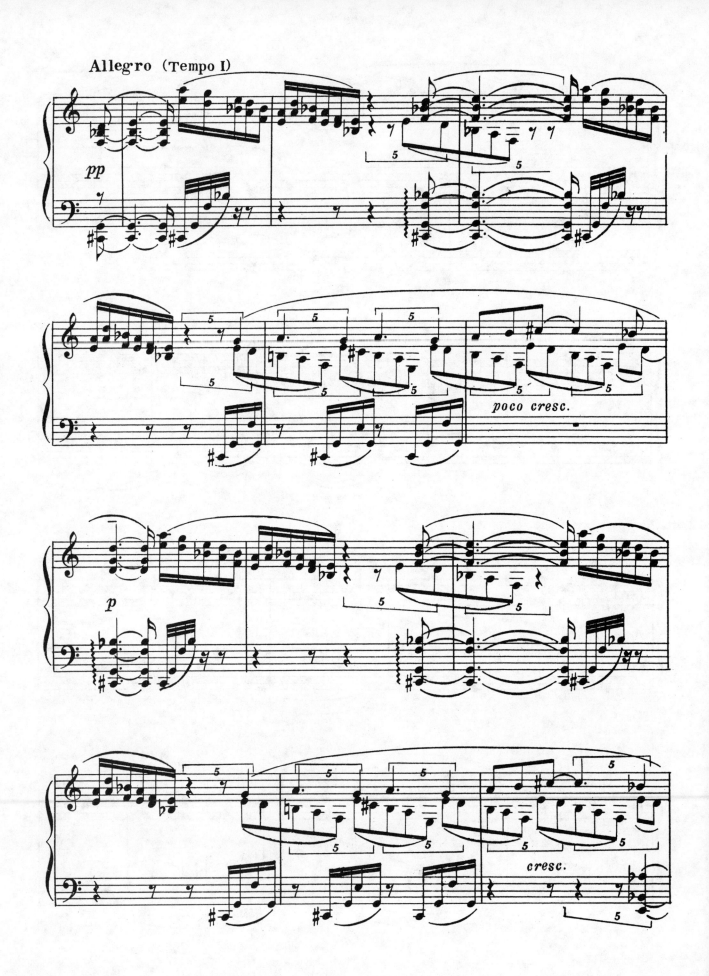

Tragique

Presto

Prestissimo

doux, languissant

Sonata No. 9 ("Black Mass"), Op. 68

Moderato quasi andante

poco rit.

204   Sonata No. 9 ("Black Mass")

molto accel.

Molto meno vivo
pur, limpide

212   Sonata No. 9 ("Black Mass")

Allegro molto

Sonata No. 10, Op. 70

220 Sonata No. 10

Puissant, radieux

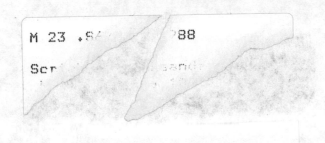

M 23 .84   ?88

Scr   sandr